Quick and Easy
Trompe L'Oeil

Acknowledgements

I would like to thank all the customers and colleagues of "English Home" who encouraged me during the realization of this manual, in particular, Cristina Ungoni for her help in the design and graphics sector.
A special thank you to all the members of "Associazione degli Artigiani dell'Ogettistica," whose works are presented in this book, with a special mention for Miata Marcolini and Maria Rigolone. My particular thanks goes to Adrian Pranzo whose works can be found on pages: 21, 36-37, 38-39, 42-43, 57, 58-59, 74, 132-133.
I would also like to thank the atelier "Arredare" (Milan) for the settings with hand painted pieces of furniture.
Merit goes to Gabrialla Gallerani for the extremely interesting 'Poulet' illustrations on the furniture illustrated in chapter "Artist Trompe L'oeil."
A thank you to Azienda Prodotti Artistici APA of Bologna.
A thank you also to Michele Loseto, Via Col Moschin 5, Milan, who supplied the trompe l'oeils on pages 13, 15, 98-99, 106-107.
I thank my mother Shelley for the trust that she has constantly shown me and the words of encouragement offered me.

Editor: Cristina Sperandeo
Photography: Piero Baguzzi
Graphic Design and Layout: Paola Masero and Ameila Verga
Translation: Chaia Tarsia

Library of Congress Cataloging-in-Publication Data Available

10 9 8 7 6 5 4 3 2 1

Published by Sterling Publishing Company, Inc.
387 Park Avenue South, New York, N.Y. 10016
First published in Italy by RCS Libri S.p.A.
Under the title Trompe L'oeil
© 1997 RCS Libri
Distributed in Canada by Sterling Publishing
c/o Canadian Manda Group, One Atlantic Avenue, Suite 105
Toronto, Ontario, Canada M6K 3E7
Distributed in Great Britain and Europe by Cassell PLC
Wellington House, 125 Strand, London WC2R 0BB, England
Distributed in Australia by Capricorn Link (Australia) Pty Ltd.
P.O. Box 6651, Baulkham Hills, Business Centre, NSW 2153, Australia
Printed in China

Sterling ISBN 0-8069-7138-X

Quick and Easy Trompe L'Oeil

*Decorative Painting on
Walls, Furniture, Frames & More*

Jocelyn Kerr Holding

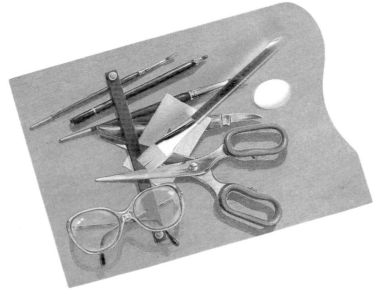

Sterling Publishing Co., Inc.
New York

TABLE OF CONTENTS

PREFACE

There are various ways of approaching the technique we call trompe l'oeil (i.e. tricks of the eye). One of these, both the most widespread and the most off putting, is that of an almost reverential regard for this art method. This can even lead to an almost blank refusal to "try one's hand" with pencils and colors. Those who have this approach are the ones who think "I can't draw, therefore I'll never be able to learn the trompe l'oeil technique". Which, however, is never quite a hundred percent true.

Then there are those who are naturally talented and are consequently perfectly able to reproduce any subject on any kind of surface and, as if that weren't enough, with great graphic precision and taste in colors too.

Finally, there are the "brave" ones. Generally self-taught, these people possess an extremely precious quality: the unfailing desire to impress their personality on a white surface through an original interpretation of a scenario, whether imaginary or real.

But no matter what category one falls into, to involve and trick the eye it is essential to follow the laws of perspective and have some bent for copying, to study proportions carefully, and to have a strong desire to give vent to one's creativity through the means made available by art.

The scenarios to be painted may originate from landscapes or glimpses of real life, seen as if from a window and reproduced as if in a picture. Magic intervenes the very moment we decide to give real dimension to these images and frame them with architectonic elements. These elements are like an imaginary bridge; they help us to leave reality behind and to enter an imaginary world.

There is one thing we must never forget, however, when dealing with the trompe l'oeil technique, and that is that the wall, the material support of our work, must be "pulled down" and disappear completely, and in its place must surface the scene we want to give life to.

JOCELN KERR HOLDING

THE ORIGINS OF TROMPE L'OEIL

During the Renaissance period, numerous workshops arose in Italy in which artisans took on young apprentices keen to learn the art of wall decorating and to make their living of it. The interest shown for the trompe l'oeil technique today mainly stems, more than from professional reasons, from the wish to cultivate a gratifying and creative hobby. In 2000 AC, the Egyptians firmly believed that decorating the walls of the tombs of their loved ones with reproductions of the customs and habits typical of their age could provide for the dead a kind of passport to eternal life.

In 700 AC, the Etruscans painted typical "Greek" scenes on the walls of their tombs for this very same reason.

The first reproductions of landscapes, no longer for religious ends, but painted purely for the sake of decoration, appeared between 200 and 700 AC in Pompeii. Wealthy Roman families commissioned painters to decorate the walls of their homes with landscapes and architectonic scenarios, where columns which seemed to recede, "running" towards the back of the picture. And it was precisely thanks to their being in accordance with the laws of perspective that these works of art were able to create the magical illusion of a three dimensional effect.

THE POWER OF PERSPECTIVE

We don't know exactly where the Romans got to in their studies on the laws of perspective, but the ruins at Pompeii have shown us that at that time there already existed the first basic laws on perspective, with a single flight point from which the lines defining depth branched off.

The advent of Christianity gave little thrust to the development of wall decorating, especially as very often the symbolic-religious value of the painting by reason of the importance of the message, exceeded quality and executive technique.

When Giotto appeared on the artistic scene in 1300, the Trompe L'oeil technique made a leap forward towards realistic reproduction. The artist carried out a series of wall decorations in the Basilica of Saint Francis in Assisi, in which he depicted the main events in the Saint's life.

Giotto was a definite break with the past by the way he added movement and expression to his mural work: the scenes at Assisi, in fact, are extremely real and the characters seem to be almost alive.

In 1400 Masaccio, another leading artist on the stage of Italian humanism painting, was able to appreciate Giotto's naturalistic approach and to develop it further.

He went beyond the Gothic style, which at that time prevailed throughout Europe, and carried out a full fledged in-depth study on perspective. Since then, the main purpose of the use of light and shade has been to give volume to space.

Attempts at recreating the impression of space on a flat surface, such as a painting, succeeded magnificently a hundred years later in the works of Andrea Mantegna, which depict the members of the Gonzaga Family in their home in Mantua.

(On the left, a detail of the trompe l'oeil fresco by Paolo Veronese, depicting a young girl at the door. It is exhibited at Villa Barbaro, Maser, near Treviso,. XVI century).

Looking out from a balcony of a painted cupola, princes and angels stand out against the sky within a framework which recreates a perfectly three dimensional illusion. Leonardo's Last Supper, of the same period, is a perfect example of the application of the laws of perspective and a complement to his incredible mastery in recreating true emotions on the faces of his characters.

The 16th Century, the century of the Renaissance, one of the most important ages for Italian culture, brought with it such a wealth of talent which is still remembered today with much wonder thanks to the most beautiful frescoes ever to have been painted. Two artists in particular dominated the scene: Raffaello Sanzio and Michelangelo Buonarotti. Raffaello painted "The School of Athens" in the Vatican rooms, where the fathers of the church meet the ancient philosophers, some of whom are Heraclitus, Euclid and Pythagoras. High lacunar arcades give the painting its perspective depth, while the scene is animated by vivacious groups of disciples surrounding the philosophers. Michelangelo considered himself to be first and foremost a sculptor, at least until 1508, the year in which Pope Julius XI commissioned him to paint the twelve apostles on a vault of the Sistine Chapel.

Spurred on by the prospect of painting the entire ceiling, Michelangelo soon mastered the art of frescoes. It took him four years to complete his masterpiece, The Creation of Man, which covers the whole vault of the chapel. Around 1555, in the second half of the Renaissance period, wall decorating became popular in Venice too, thanks to Paolo Veronese, a rising artist and a favorite with the Doge. Veronese was called by the Doge to embellish the wall and ceilings of the Doge's Palace in Venice with his glimpses of every day life.

ARCHITECTONIC ELEMENTS AMPLIFY SPACE

But the most original work signed by Veronese was the one commissioned from him by the Italian architect Andrea Palladio for Villa Barbaro, at Maser; a neo-classical building which Palladio designed for his brothers Marcantonio and Daniele Barbaro. In this trompe l'oeil-style fresco, a life-sized young girl, the daughter of one of the architect's brothers, peeps with incredible realism from behind a door set slightly ajar. Two hundred years later Tiepolo, while still maintaining the traditional Venetian line begun by Veronese, added great color and baroque richness to his paintings. Among these, to be remembered is his favorite subject: Cleopatra who seems to "emerge" from the walls of Labia Palace, serene and majestic like the city of Venice.

Throughout the ages, and right down to the 20th century, trompe l'oeil has been considered as one of the most interesting forms of decorating. We too, today, just like the inhabitants of Pompeii, like to treat ourselves to "playing" with illusion, to reproducing on the walls of our homes scenes from every day life, as well as rustic objects, as if they were real, in order to excite a sense of well-being, harmony and peace.

On the next page: a famous painting by René Magritte entitled "La lumette d'approche" (1963). Magritte, a twentieth century artist, used the technique most often as well as using it most originally.

LOOKING FOR A SUBJECT

LONG NARROW CORRIDORS

Long, narrow corridors can pose a real problem from the moment that their side walls are really nothing but enormous bare, white spaces. This can be modified by painting a beautiful panoramic view on the two longest walls, for example. Also amusing could be "inventing" doors and windows on the side walls of a long, narrow corridor, at the end of which a window or a balcony door opens. The most important thing is that the decoration on both walls be perfectly in line with their surroundings.

CORNERS

Decorating walls that converge into corners is no simple task. In this case a creeper would be the ideal subject to draw in order to make this "difficult" point more pleasant to look at.

NICHES AND RECESSES

Instead of filling these spaces with tailor-made bookshelves or wardrobes, why not opt for a bush of roses obliquely creeping up the walls, with fountains painted on either side just before the recess. This decoration is definitely an innovative solution which will help to make a difficult-shaped niche blend in nicely with the context of the room in which it is situated.

A WINDOW OVERLOOKING AN EXTERNAL WALL

A window overlooking an external wall, for example a very high fencing wall, is decidedly an "unlucky" window. Painting an imaginary scene on this "claustrophobic" surface, exactly in line with the window, "opens" this closed space, giving a new vitality to the view.

AN UNDESIRED PROJECTION

"To transform" the three surfaces of a projecting wall, a 'continual' scene is recommended, in other words one which runs along all three surfaces. The projecting form itself will give a three dimensional effect to the painting.

Depicted below is an example of how trompe l'oeil can complement the furniture of a room: this partition wall between the kitchen and the dining room was painted with a classical motif, thus giving character to a space otherwise difficult to enhance.

IN MORPHEUS' ARMS

The trompe l'oeil technique is very much used and loved to decorate the wall behind the bed. The illusion thus created will automatically become the focus point of the room. To justify it being in such an important position, however, the fresco will have to be very convincing.

THE BATHROOM

Very often the wall surface around the bath tub or the shower is not taken into the same consideration as the rest of the bathroom. An architectonic scene, with columns, capitals and so on, is the best way to lead the eye beyond the limited space created by real walls because it helps to give greater height and depth to the bathroom.

CEILINGS

Painting a ceiling requires a lot of effort. The difficulty, however, lies not so much in the artistic ability as in the physical strength needed to stand for hours on end on a ladder, constantly facing upwards and with one arm stretched. After a while this uncomfortable position could provoke unbearable cramps in the upper limbs. We therefore recommend choosing extremely simple motifs, such as clouds, flower or fruit wreaths, or perhaps two cherubs.

WARDROBES

Why not give personality to a large wardrobe and decorate its doors with floral motifs or with a "continual" scene on its whole front surface. If, instead, you would rather a simpler decoration, then a corner motif could fill the contours of the door with great effect.

ATTICS

The "irregular" spaces of an attic can also be transformed into scenic views: for example a balcony overlooking a distant, hilly landscape. To give greater credibility to the illusion of three dimensionality, try painting a winding road gradually disappearing into the background.

TO INTERRUPT A VERY LARGE ROOM

Trompe l'oeil libraries painted on projecting walls, or on other types of surface, give rise to a characteristic setting reminiscent of theatre wings. Personalize the shelves by arranging objects of your choice in between the books.

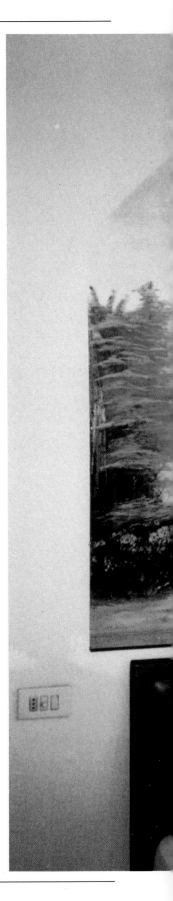

A niche above the head board could become the room's strong point if adequately decorated with a relaxing and dream-inducing trompe l'oeil motif, like the one depicted in the photo.

THE BASICS OF TROMPE L'OEIL

MATERIALS

To obtain the maximum result from the colors you will be using as well as from all auxiliary products necessary to dilute, soften, accelerate or slow down the drying process, we recommend you experiment first with oils, creams and gels, here subdivided according to their use. These also help to create "special effects" and allow for the standard procedures to be applied, which would otherwise be very difficult to do.

PREPARING THE SURFACE

Although it isn't mandatory to prepare the area being painted, we recommend preparing the base with an isolated synthetic resin-based product called Primal, as this makes the act of spreading colors easier and gives the end result an even effect. This material stays constant even in temperature changes. It is also an excellent covering product for walls. Acrylic resins used as binding agents for pigments may also be used for the background. Should you want to work on wood, cardboard or plastic, then the surface must be treated with cementite or with several coats of white acrylic.

RETARDING MEDIUM FOR ACRYLIC COLORS

Glycol oil is compatible with water-based colors and helps to slow down the extremely rapid drying process typical of acrylic colors, as well as to render a color more flexible. As an additive, this oil is suitable for color fragmentation techniques, such as marbling, artificial wood, malachite, etc.

ACRYLICRE SIN IN EMULSION

Suitable for decorative arts and trompe l'oeil, acrylic resin suspends pure pigments in powder.

GEL MEDIUM

An alkyd resin-based solvent, this gel is used to soften the consistency of alkyd colors and to transform them into a translucent, slippery paste. There are two different types available density-wise: gel 200, decidedly the least dense of the two and suitable for the fine arts and trompe l'oeil technique, and gel 300 used for sponging, ragging and stippling. The latter gel is used both to increase the volume of an acrylic color, making it similar to a bright and transparent paint, and to slow down the drying process of alkyd colors.

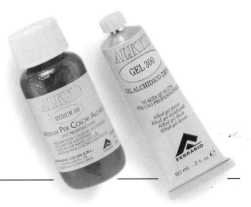

BRUSHES

As basic equipment, three brushes are enough, but if you wish to invest in a complete set you should choose the following six types:
N° 1 2 cm wide brush with long, flat, square-shaped bristles in synthetic fibers;
N° 1 1.5 cm wide flat tipped brush in synthetic fibers;
N° 2 bristle brushes with very fine tips, '0' and '00'.
Characteristics: Synthetic fibers are soft and elastic, while bristles are inclined to be more rigid. They hold the color better, however. Some spatulas will be needed for measuring and mixing the colors.

COLORS

ALKYD COLORS
These colors are of vegetable extraction and come suspended in an oil-based synthetic resin. Their recent success springs from their rapid drying powers, for although oil-based, they dry much quicker than traditional oil colors. They also offer an alkyd gel able to soften their consistency and give luminosity and brilliancy.

OIL COLORS
Their composition is similar to that of alkyd colors, but they also contain an oily vegetable base combined with a synthetic resin. They dry in 24-48 hours. Their high content of finely distributed pure pigments makes them particularly suitable for painting on fabric and other fine art work.

ACRYLIC COLORS
These are water-based and come suspended in an acrylic synthetic resin, dissolvable in water, but water proof once dry. This rapid drying power of acrylics can pose a problem if the color needs lengthy modelling. In this event, the color has to be mixed with a solving agent so as to prolong flexibility.

PURE PIGMENTS IN POWDER
Pigments in powder, traditionally used for frescoes and restoration work, can be mixed in various ways, according to the need to use a creamy substance or a less dense one. Pigments are usually suspended in an acrylic resin or a water-based emulsion.

"BEHIND" THE COLOR

THE CHROMATIC WHEEL

The chromatic wheel is made up of three primary colors (red, yellow and blue) and three secondary ones (green, orange, violet). Primary colors are free from any color mixing. Secondary colors are those rising from mixing two primary colors in equal parts. In fact:

red + yellow = orange
yellow + blue = green
red + blue = violet

When beginning to use colors for a certain goal, you must learn to distinguish them by the names of their respective pigments. For example 'brown' *is a generic term, as it does not refer to a pigment but indicates a chromatic shade, without being more specific. The so called 'browns' which vary are distinguished by their pigments: natural Umber, Van Dyke brown and Burnt Sienna.*

The primary pigments or colors are:
* *Cadmium yellow*
* *Prussian blue*
* *Carmine red*

The secondary colors are.
* *Violet*
* *Carmine orange*
* *Chrome green*

DARKENING OR LIGHTENING COLORS

Though usually used to darken colors, black accentuates the primary color present in the tint to be darkened, since it contains all three primary colors. This reaction produces a secondary color and not, as can be imagined, the darker one. For example: yellow + blue = green, red + black = brown.
To darken colors, therefore, their corresponding shades on the *chromatic wheel must be used, and not black. To darken yellow, we must use its correspondent on the chromatic scale, which is violet: yellow + violet = dark yellow. To darken red we use the respective correspondent, which is green: red + green = dark green, russet. To darken blue, we use orange, and so on.*
Though we often use white to lighten colors, it must not be forgotten that this *color reduces the color's gloss and makes it more opaque. Yellow is the ideal alternative, but only when the color to be lightened does not already contain large doses of yellow. To lighten green, for example, which already contains yellow, we use white: chrome green + white. To lighten the chrome oxide, instead, we can happily use yellow: chrome oxide + yellow.*

HIDING A GAS OR ELECTRICITY METER

The doors of a cupboard open and display clothes of various kinds and colors, stacked away on two shelves. Observe the position of the items on the top shelf, which hang on purpose to give the composition an *idea of movement, as otherwise it would be too static. To create the contrast between the clothes which receive direct light and those that on the contrary reflect it, numerous different shades of white have been used.*

WARM COLORS

Warm colors are mainly made up of reds and yellows. This series of warm colors is suitable for "describing" a bright, sunny afternoon, a sunset or dawn.

Warm colors remain such, even if mixed with black, blue or purple. To tone down "fire red" and lighten it, it is sufficient to add a little white.

Now try and make your own pool of warm colors, combining ochre yellow, natural

Sienna, cadmium yellow, Burnt Sienna, Vermilion, Pozzuoli, Naples yellow.

COOL COLORS

Cool colors are less "passionate", more "distant" and more relaxing. The light reflecting off cool colors can be compared to the extremely bright light of the high sun reflecting off the zenith, or to twilight, or again to the light of a grey autumn evening.

The colors coming out of the tubes below are in part made up of pure pigments, while others are a combination of two hues. From left to right:
Viridian Green, Chrome Oxide, Emerald green, Cerulean Blue, Prussian Blue, Cadmium Green (yellowy), Light Blue Turquoise, Cyan Blue, Ultramarine Blue, Cobalt Blue with Emerald Green. Why not get a palette ready with cool colors: some pure ones and others obtained by mixing two hues together.

NEUTRAL COLORS

As we know, if we mix the three primary colors yellow, blue and red, we obtain black. Neutral grey, the color used to reproduce shadows, is made up of the three primary colors mixed together, this time in unequal parts. Once we have obtained the grey, however, it must be finished off with a color of the object to be shaded. For example, to obtain shadows in compositions which are sunny and rich in warm colors, the grey will be mixed with Sienna, Ochre, and Magenta. For colder landscapes, usually winter ones, the shadows will have, for example, a tinge of grey/blue,

grey/olive green, etc. Neutral colors lend themselves perfectly to creating city views, Ashlar-work, granite, the half light, industrial scenes and other cases where shadows extend over a wide area, under a bridge or along a lane. It often happens that in the range of available colors, that certain shade indispensable for creating the right atmosphere doesn't exist. By mixing colors together, however, we can get the particular nuance we want and turn our composition, still a little unsatisfactory, into a work rich in atmosphere and even improve the perception of volume. Let us consider, for

example, the various types of green pigments and their effect: Terre Verte is dark; Sage Green normally needs white to be more luminous; Chrome Oxide is a bluish green and doesn't need to be mixed with other colors; Emerald Green is suitable for depicting the sea, but is too blue to represent classical grass green, and in this case it has to be mixed with a yellowish green; Cadmium Green is a yellowish green which, when mixed with burnt Sienna gives a decidedly winterish rusty green; Chrome Green is a warm, yellowish green.

LAWS OF PERSPECTIVE

A trompe l'oeil scene must be centered around a point, called the focal point. The perspective project built up in accordance with the focal point and its flight lines highlights a visual range. This visual range will then be developed and particularly emphasised. Three visual ranges can be constructed:
• Foreground
• Middle distance
• Background

THE BACKGROUND

The background could be defined as the field of vision furthest from the observer. The background has two centers of interest: the "near" background and the "distant" one. In the former are to be found the outlines just beyond the middle distance, and in the distant one those which converge with the sky on the horizon furthest away.

THE MIDDLE DISTANCE

A figure of significant interest may be placed in the middle distance which is half way between the foreground and the background. Automatically, the eye will look for further visual information beyond the middle distance and will then alight on the outlines in the background.

FOREGROUND

When the object is represented as if it were seen from below, the foreground widens and "rises" up to the horizon line. This widening of the field nearest the observer causes an accentuation of the details in the foreground, while the particulars to be found on the furthest planes will be merely hinted at.
If, on the contrary, the object in the foreground is at the observer's eye level, it is this that will appear most clearly; at the same time, however, it will be necessary to integrate the object in the foreground in the middle distance and background, defining the shape of these last two, but downplaying the details.

The laws of perspective do not only hold for architecture but must also be applied to small drawings, whether of objects or people.

THE VIEW POINT

The view point is the point from where the observer beholds the scene:
• A high horizon line corresponds to a low view point
• A low horizon line corresponds to a high view point

A low view point (the observer is seated) widens the field closest to the observer, filling the scene from the foreground right to the background. A view point at the beholder's eye-level will divide into equal parts the foreground, the middle distance and the background. A high view point will establish a low horizon, projecting into view the middle distance and the background together with a good part of the sky.

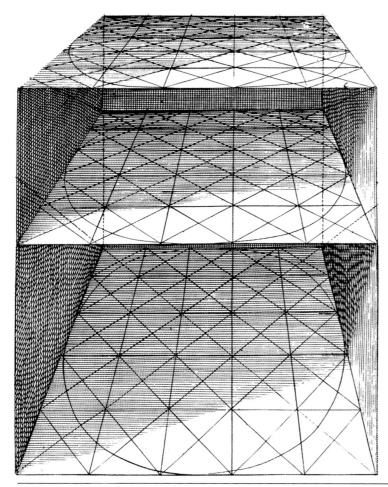

PERSPECTIVE LINES

The diagonal lines which converge towards the accidental point or view point give the impression of depth.

H – horizon
V.P. – view point
A.P. - accidental point
P.L – perspective lines (converging point)

Oryon

FRONTAL PERSPECTIVE

This perspective requires only one A.P. (V.P.) placed along the horizon line.

1) First draw the horizon H

2) Position the A.P./V.P

3) Draw a square and name its four sides AB BC CD DA

4) Draw the perspective lines which branch off from the angles A, B, C, D so that they converge on the F.P.

5) Draw a second square behind the first, and name its four sides EFF, FG, GH, IJ, placing the angles EF-GH along the perspective lines.

The cube is seen from a frontal perspective. If you try to imagine that instead of a cube there is a rock, it will be easier to perceive the three dimensions.

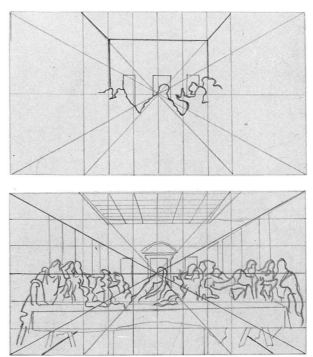

A DRIVE

The view beyond the iron gate was constructed on a frontal perspective. As is typical with the trompe l'oeil technique, the trees lining the sides of the drive converge on an imaginary focal point in the center of the drawing. As they recede into the background, the trees become increasingly smaller, with the distance between one tree and the other gradually diminishing.

THE LAST SUPPER

The project of The Last Supper shows a frontal perspective with a focal point situated exactly behind the figure of Christ. A second rectangle frames the central section of the painting, giving the possibility of inserting the accidental points, which put the beamed ceiling into perspective.

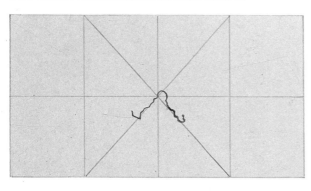

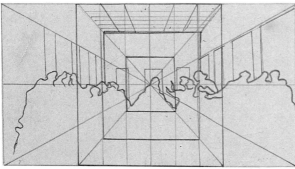

ACCIDENTAL PERSPECTIVE

There are always two accidental points in an accidental perspective. In this case, the subject is always seen from an angle. To draw a cube with an accidental perspective, first sketch a horizon line with two accidental points: A.P.1 and A.P.2. Draw the line closest to you, named AB. Then draw the perspective lines branching off from A and B, making them converge in both A.P.1 and A.P.2. Now draw the faces of the cube sketching out the lines CA, AE, DB and BF.

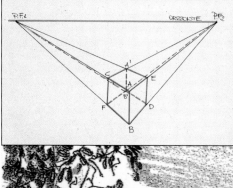

AERIAL PERSPECTIVE

Aerial perspective is used when a view is reproduced as if seen from, for example, the second floor of a building, a terrace or a roof, or from a line horizontally parallel to the ground level on which the beholder stands.

This perspective has three A.P., two of which are situated on the horizon line, while the third is positioned on the line parallel to the horizon.

Repeat the procedure with which accidental perspective is drawn, leading the perspective lines from points ABC to A.P.3.

Aerial perspective is used in those cases in which the aim is to give to the trompe l'oeil a greater feeling of space and depth.

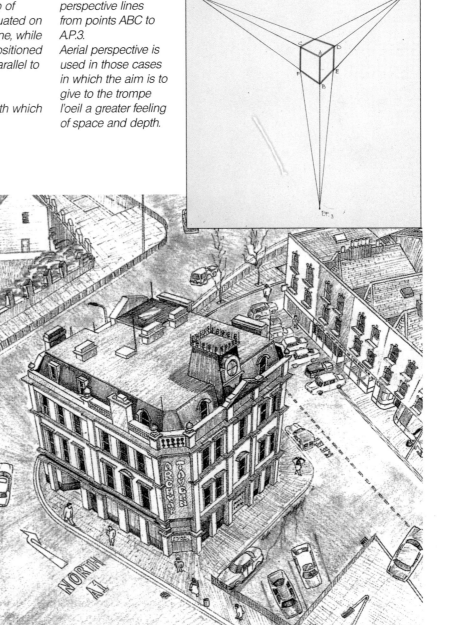

FISH BOWL

The gold fish on this tray have been reproduced with incredible realism by the artist. The horizontal perspective gives depth to the painting. In order to recreate the typical distortion of lines through water, the artist immersed a cage into the bath tub and then carefully observed the irregular shapes that were thus formed.

ADRIANA PRANZO

The trompe l'oeil creations by this artist are the result of paying particular attention to detail. Before starting to paint, in fact, the artist carries out an in-depth study on the shadows of the composition as well as on the shape of the object and its location, breaking it up into small parts. Adriana Pranzo is famed in the trompe l'oeil field; in her artistic career, she has collected a series of prizes and acknowledgements and has taken part in many national and international exhibitions and competitions.

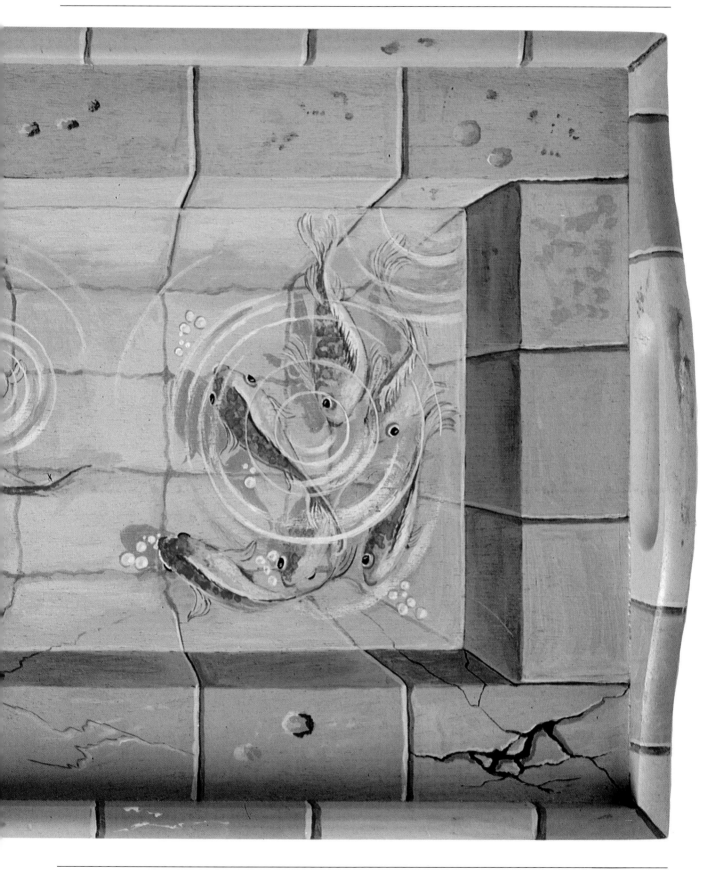

"TRICKS" OF PERSPECTIVE

The flat surface of a wall, of a table top, of a sheet of paper and so on have only two dimensions: length and width. The third measurement becomes evident when we "pull down" this surface and we *"make our way" into the space thus created. From this moment there exists the illusion of depth: nearness and distance.*

Near + far = depth of field.

To give the illusion of depth, there are three "strategies" which can be used to create space :

1. Superimposition
2. Contrast
3. Proportion

1. SUPERIMPOSITION

Objects put naturally in perspective are perceived at different levels: foreground, middle distance, etc. *The objects will look as if they overlap one another, therefore: near ... distant... very distant.*

A CHEST OF DRAWERS

In this original painting, some objects randomly overlap others. All the objects, conceived as elements in their own right, occupy a precise space. Every single one of them, however, was drawn proportionally with regard to the others and then, according to its position, was finished off with contrasts of light and shade.

2. CONTRASTS

When we overlap elements, we must create contrast. Therefore the objects in the foreground will be dark, the ones a little more distant a shade lighter and the ones furthest away very light.

TONAL VALUES

There exist an infinite number of tones which range from pure black to pure white. But to simplify the tonal spectrum we can bring these values down to 6. The art of using these values in the most appropriate manner to create the "deception" effect as well as possible depends on the ability of the artist to turn the colors of nature into different hues. We must therefore consider our eye as if it were a black and white spool of film on which images remain impressed in all their different shades: from the lightest to the darkest.

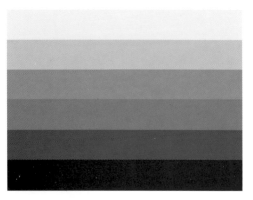

STRUGGLE

The well known theme of contrast is treated in an unusual manner: the dark hues of brown and grey strongly contrast with the white sheet of paper. Observe how in the black and white version the distinction between light and dark is even more pronounced.

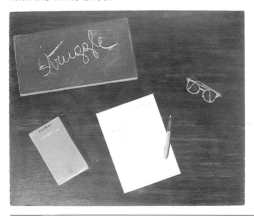

HAMSTERS

Depicted on this page are three hamsters in a cage: two in the foreground and a third one at the back. The light filtering through the cage bars illuminates the snouts of the two hamsters which are eating. The hamster in the background is illuminated by the same light, but appears to be enveloped in the semi-darkness of the depth of the cage, so its light shades are decidedly less luminous than those of the other two. To underline the existence of space behind the hamsters, the artist illuminated the top part of the inside of the cage on the right.

A CAT AND A DRAGON FLY

In the small black and white photograph below, it is possible to distinguish a certain number of shades, ten to be precise: pure white and pure black, however, are not among them. The background against which the cat is depicted is of a slightly darker color and gives the idea of there being space behind the animal. The light coming from the left illuminates the cushion and the left side of the cat's snout, the two points in the whole picture with the most light.

THE CAT AND THE BUTTERFLY

Contrast and superimposition give the cat and butterfly a three dimensional effect. The highly contrasting luminosity highlights the tail in the foreground; a less brilliant light falls on the top part of the cat's body, thus placing it in the middle distance. The butterfly was drawn last and appears to be in front of the cat. The butterfly stands out against the background thanks to the use of a medium bright shade outlining its wings.

SQUIRRELS

This is another example of a light/dark picture, all the more evident in the black and white version. Both squirrels receive the same amount of light, with a slight difference: the light illuminating the squirrel in the foreground is full and strong, while the one illuminating the squirrel at the back is darkened by the shadows inside the cage. The circle around the eyes of the squirrel in the foreground is almost white, while it is whitish grey in the second squirrel.

3. PROPORTIONS

Form + dimension = proportion. Dimensions and shapes are initially measured at a glance, with quick, mental calculations.

The question then arises how to relate the elements among themselves in order to give the proper proportion.

DIMENSIONS

How high is a tree when seen in the foreground in relation to the hills behind it? How wide is that building in relation to its height? Before drawing the chosen objects, it is necessary to find out what their approximate sizes are so as to be able to reproduce them in proportion. A trick of the trade lies in measuring the height of the objects, whatever the distance that separates you from them, by holding a pencil at arm's length and eye-level, in front of the object you intend to reproduce. Using a pencil as a unit of measure for each object making up your composition will make it possible to compare the objects to one another and to draw them in their right proportions.

SHAPES

As Cezanne affirmed, all the shapes present in nature are modelled on the structure of three main solids: a cube, a cylinder and a sphere. Therefore, if the structure of the objects are drawn first, using their geometric solid as a starting point, then the artist will be able to obtain greater field depth.

IN CONCLUSION

Elements in the foreground are reproduced life-size; objects in the middle distance are smaller compared to those in the foreground, while the objects in the background are tiny because they are furthest away. Before starting remember to:
1. Decide on the point which needs highlighting;
2. Establish the view point, that is the point from where the observer beholds the scene;
3. Pinpoint a horizon line according to the view point.

THE VIEW POINT
Is a dot on the horizon line defining the position of the beholder, and from which the visual rays branch off.

THE ACCIDENTAL POINT
Consists in one or more dots on the horizon line, on which the perspective lines converge and possibly disappear.

The photo below is a fine example of a study on shapes and proportions. This painting, by the great artist René Magritte, is entitled: "La clef de verre" (1959).

TECHNIQUES

A trompe l'oeil painting may be made in various ways. Even though it is without doubt a free hand reproduction of reality, it is also true that ever since Man started experimenting with wall decorating techniques, he has always endeavored to come up with as may methods as possible to achieve this aim without difficulty. The following pages explain some important tricks of the trade.

THE PERFORATING TECHNIQUE

This technique was first used during the Renaissance period to reproduce, faithfully and down to the slightest detail, the scene to be painted. First of all, the outline of the object is drawn on a sheet of tracing paper and then lots of small holes are perforated all round it. Using carbon powder, the painting is then "dusted" on the wall, which means that the spaces delimited by the guidelines are painted in and contrasts of light and dark added.

1 Pierce the contours of the drawing on both the photocopy and the tracing paper.

2 *Use a pad of carbon powder to dab on the tracing paper along the holes. Dusting must be carried out with a partly dabbing and partly wiping motion.*

3 *Having taken note of the various levels of light and dark on the photocopy, proceed to painting in the drawing, making sure to respect the areas defined by the guiding lines.*

A CHINESE VASE

From this rough draft, the artist created a delightful Chinese vase, simulating a shelf as its resting place.

PROJECTION

Projection acquired significant importance in the trompe l'oeil technique when portrait artists began to think they could carry out reproductions that almost resembled photographs. With the dimensions desired, the slide of the object to be reproduced is projected on the wall. The perspective lines are drawn by the photograph itself. The scene is therefore painted over it. At any point, the slide may be re-projected on the painting to correct any details.

A WINDOW OVERLOOKING A PARK

This trompe l'oeil is extremely suitable for beginners. Try to reproduce this window overlooking a park, with a path winding off into the horizon. The use of acrylic colors will allow you to achieve a soft, water-color effect. Use a retarding medium to slow down the quick drying process so typical of these colors.
1. Using a ruler and set square, draw a window and divide it into six equal parts. With the help of a drawing curve, round off the two top parts of the window. Draw the landscape free hand, remembering to follow the main laws of perspective.
2. Color the window using Umber lightened with white and then, using the same Umber, darken the wooden grooves of the window. Attach paper adhesive around the contours to prevent the colors from smudging.

3. Draw the landscape in all the six parts of the window bearing in mind all the while the end result. The colors we suggest you use for the landscape are green Chrome Oxide, Yellow Ochre, Umber and Burnt Sienna. White will serve to lighten wherever necessary. Shade the handle of the window with pearled grey, lightening it in the center to give volume. Color the sky with a very light blue, almost white around the trees and towards the horizon. Give a slight touch of color to the wall bricks. Color the stone pavement with very light grey, accentuating around the edges of each single tile.

FREE HAND DRAWING

Painting a real scene or a series of real objects free hand is often considered as "copying from reality". In a way, trying to faithfully reproduce what we see can be seen as copying, but it can also be seen as a way of "interpreting". Placed before an object, in fact, each one of us will produce a slightly different version of the real model. We all tend to personalize our own creations, as the image is interpreted according to our sensitivity, habits and general view of life. Some people use colors in a particularly vivacious way, while others use the bare minimum. In one composition a particular detail is highlighted, while in another that same detail may be only slightly hinted at. What we generally look for in a trompe l'oeil is the maximum likeness to the object being reproduced. Very often, however, when we observe a stream flowing between rocks, tree tops rising above shadowy woods, or waves breaking on a beach, these scenes exercise such power on our emotions as to influence significantly the way in which we reproduce the view.

KEYS

Realistically hanging in a wooden closet, these keys seem to be dangling slightly thanks to the particular attention the artist has given to shading. Given that the inside of the closet was not drawn with much depth, a sufficient amount of light illuminates the background, while the dark corner on the left-hand side suggests a source of light from the right.

A PALETTE

Every day objects are randomly arranged on the palette of an artist. No perspective laws govern this painting. The illusion has been entirely obtained through the use of strong contrasts of light and shade, very pronounced under the scissors and less so under the pair of glasses. This trompe l'oeil was made by Adriana Pranzo.

FLOWERS

If we intend to reproduce a garden without adding too many details, the important thing will be to manage to create the "impression" of a garden full of flowers.

1. The first brush-strokes determine the direction as well as the color.
2. Now, with touches of pink, add the first nuance of color to the flowers, dotting some parts of the drawing with a darker shade. Then *strengthen and elaborate on the chromatic structure of the painting by creating dark and light points.*
3. The end of the garden is defined with dashes of dark green and green blue shading.
4. Lastly, touches of dark red give the idea of small areas of shade, which represent the bloom, while lighter touches will give the impression that the flowers are lit by the sun.

CLOUDS

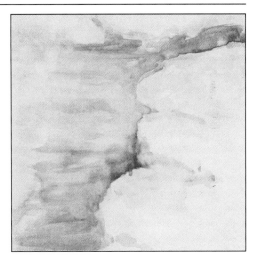

Clouds don't usually have forms because they are constantly changing according to the air currents. The outlines of your clouds, therefore, must be soft and indefinite.

1. Start by sketching out indefinite shapes in light blue and almost white.

2. Give the sketched shapes more volume and increase the contrast of the chiaroscuro.

3. Strengthen the color and shape, always bearing in mind that the sky is light at the horizon and darker close to the zenith.

4. Clouds, as well as other trompe l'oeil elements, are three dimensional. Choose that part of the cloud to give light to and color it with lighter tones. The bottom part of the clouds is generally shaded as it gets less light.

TREES

If trees are not in the foreground, we never see them as detailed forms, but merely as blurred outlines painted with touches of light and dark green. The direction and thickness of the branches is chosen according to their growth. It is necessary to give the trees a strong and vigorous shape at the base, adding a knot-type effect that is typical of wood. The sun illuminates only part of the foliage, creating a contrast of light and shade, essential if you want to give dramatic power to the painting.

PHOTOCOPIES

An alternative: the same photocopies enlarged can be used as the base of the drawing. The original Florentine frame photographed in this sequence is no other than an enlarged photocopy glued directly on to the wall and then painted in, using three or four nuances of the same color.

1 *Make an enlarged photocopy of the frame with a professional photocopying machine, so that even the smallest details, essential to render the shaded chiaroscuro effect directly on the paper, will show up. Cut out the frame with a pair of small scissors and glue it to the wall.*

2 *Give a light coat of the main color over the whole surface to camouflage the photocopy.*

3 Now paint the light and dark nuances, following the tones on the photocopy. Mix four shades of the same color together to reproduce the original tonal variations: light, medium dark and very dark.

PICTORIAL ART

Pictorial paintings in almost naïf style are extremely popular for their vivacious colors and are perfect for decorating different types of rooms: flower bouquets or soft Persian cats personalize a room, leading the eye straight to where they have been painted.

A group of objects outlined in wood and then painted in create an extremely colourful focus point in a sitting room.

A niche with a flower bouquet painted in trompe l'oeil style highlights in an amusing way an otherwise forgotten corner.

A bunch of Spring flowers, a Chinese vase and a curious-looking cat give life to a niche or a small recess.

Real or Unreal? The wall paper depicting a library, suitable for camouflaging the door of a real library, and the central panel are both trompe l'oeil.

PAINTED STONES

Painted stones are a novelty in the trompe l'oeil world, and their charm depends on their three dimensional form and their decorative versatility: they can, in fact, be used as paperweights, doorstoppers or as simple knick-knacks.

The large, flat, round stones, which can be found on beaches or along a riverbank, are the ideal base for a trompe l'oeil. Use oil colors to decorate them. To obtain a natural effect once the work is done, do not polish the stone, but leave it opaque.

DOG DOORSTOPPERS

When looking for stones, choose them according to their shape, and try to imagine mentally what object they could be used for. The photo on the left depicts an elongated stone, which gave the artist the idea of drawing on it a sausage dog.

USUAL PAPERWEIGHTS

The strange collection of objects photographed on this page will certainly strike the imagination of those of you who love painting on stones. On the stone/newspaper is depicted a crumpled sheet of newspaper. The result is such as to almost overturn the visual effect: there seems to be a real sheet of newspaper rolled into a round shape greatly resembling that of a stone.

PAINTING ON WOOD

Decorative objects we are very familiar with can be outlined in wood to then become bunches of flowers or even marbled columns on which rich bouquets tower. With a hint of ingeniousness, this column may be transformed into an umbrella stand, into the base of a lampshade, a clothes hanger or simply a decorative panel whose purpose is to hide anti-aesthetic sockets.

1. To begin with, draw the shape of the object on plywood and then start to color it in with light colors. To obtain the marbled effect use alkyd colors mixed with the appropriate gel. Use light Sienna as the main color, and lighten it with a dash of white before proceeding with Ochre Yellow, Burnt Sienna and light Umber for the marble veins. Should you have any doubts regarding the marbling technique, turn back to page 86.

2. These flowers, painted free hand, give the feeling of a space very close to virtual reality. Note how the different shades of green define the nearest and furthest planes of the bouquet.

3. With a saw, cut the wood, following the external outline of the flowers and the column.

DECORATIVE PANELS

Trompe l'oeil panels are often used as library or wardrobe doors, or as simple decorations to hide telephone sockets, gas and electricity meters, fusibles or water pipes. Subjects vary according to taste and needs. Most people choose images they are familiar with and which blend in with almost all surroundings. The painting depicted on the next page gives the illusion of space in quite a realistic manner.

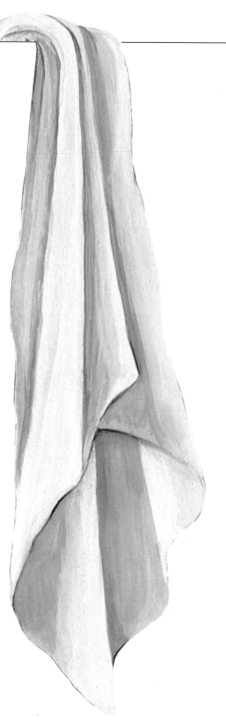

Depicted is a closet arranged with terracotta jugs. The dark shadows behind the jugs give the idea of space, while a wooden box protruding from the top shelf creates a small shadow on the surface directly below it. A French baguette can be seen on the bottom shelf and a white cloth hangs realistically over the door.

COPYING TECHNIQUES

The best technique for learning to copy natural materials such as marble, wood or precious stones is to observe carefully the color, contrasts, veins, the depth and grain of these materials. Marble veins are always diagonal, while wood grains are often vertical or circular. Both marble and wood have considerable field depth, therefore several coats of color, in light and dark tones, must be applied, and then integrated "softly" into the background.

WOOD

Copying the texture of wood is not as difficult as may first appear. To obtain the heavily streaked effect of the grains, lay one color over the other, starting from the lightest to the darkest. After each application, draw and elongate the grains with a soft paintbrush.

A PIPE

In a trompe l'oeil painting, more emphasis must be put on the chiaroscuro effect of the wood, which signals the distance or closeness of the object to a source of light, rather than on its grain. In the painting on the right, observe how the open drawer receives light on the top part of the wood. Note, however, how the same wood is much darker inside the drawer.

This piece of furniture, made originally of simple raw wood, was initially painted with colored cement and Earth Pink in order to obtain the typical color of terracotta. Then, using the acrylic colors Van Dyke Dark Brown, Burnt Sienna and Black diluted with a little retarding medium, the wood grains were created, softened at the end with a wide flat brush.

MARBLE

Obtaining a good marble effect mostly depends on the skill of the artist in moving colors on the surface and in letting them flow in various directions. The paint is then "collected" to form the veins, to "soften" and to create shadings.

If you prefer inventing your own marble, try coupling together some of the following shadings, which are typical of marble surfaces: Sienna, Burnt Sienna, Umber, Burnt Umber, terra rosa, Ochre Yellow, Payne's Grey, Terre Verte, Prussian blue, Veronese Green. Lamp bases, "high obelisks", candle holders and eggs are all very decorative objects on which you can experiment the technique of artificial marble.

MAKING ARTIFICIAL MARBLE

1 *Prepare the surface with white enamel, leave to dry and spread linen oil on the whole area to be marbled. Choose the three colors you are going to use and prepare them in three different bowls, for example Umber, Ochre Yellow and Burnt Sienna. Dab the three tones diagonally on the surface.*

2 *To tone down the color, use a thick, soft paintbrush. Scrape it diagonally on the surface.*

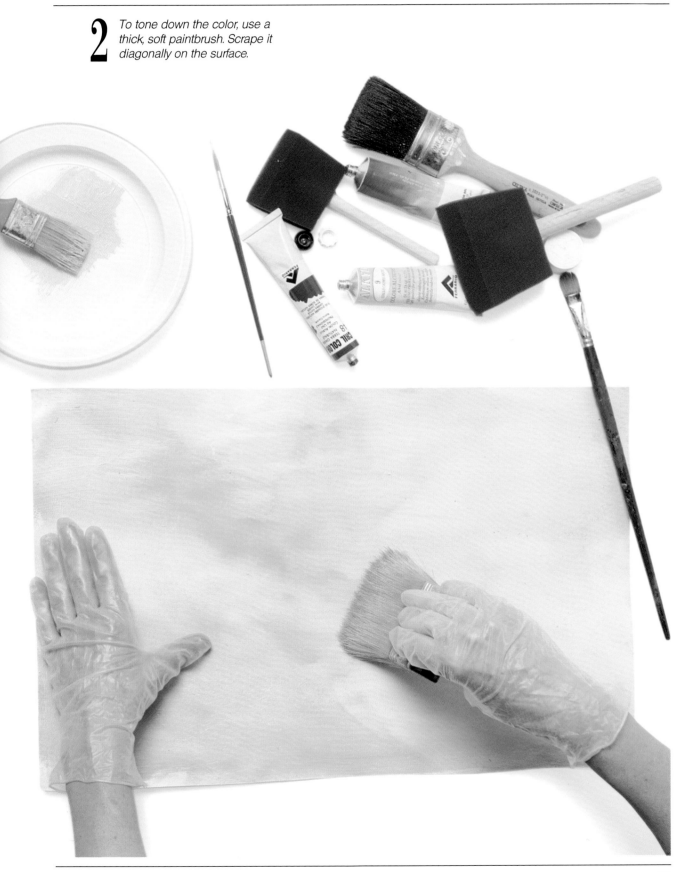

3 *Give depth to the marble by laying one color over the other. Then tone down the color towards the background.*

Depicted on the next page is a particular place mat, which was first marbled and then decorated with trompe l'oeil playing cards.

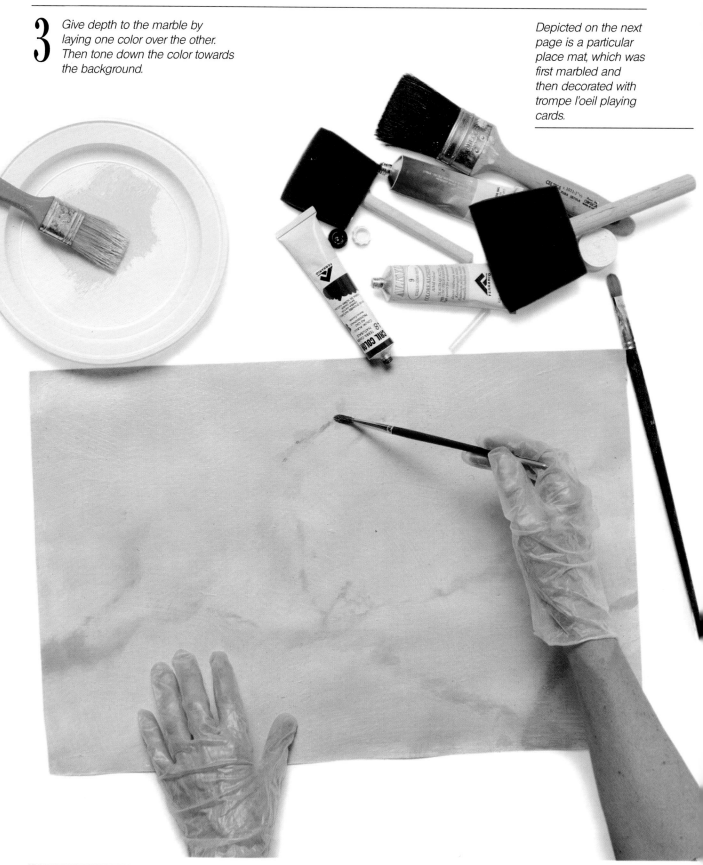

MALACHITE

Malachite has always fascinated those who like recreating stone and marble with paint. Thanks to its particular color, a classical iridescent green with its unique streaks so typical of malachite, and its ability to give movement to a room, malachite is a very popular choice when it comes to decorating the base of a lampshade.

1 *Prepare the surface paper with very light Veronese green enamel. Use three different cups to dilute it with and add a spot of gel to the three hues necessary to create the malachite effect: Veronese green, Burnt Umber and Ultramarine Blue. Dab one color over the other across the whole surface, making sure, however, that Veronese green remains the prevailing color.*

2 *Tear some cardboard into small pieces measuring about 3 x 3 cm and 5 x 5 cm.*

3 *Holding the pieces quite firmly between four fingers and your thumb, press the cardboard on the surface paper, making circular motions. This is the way to create malachite crystals.*

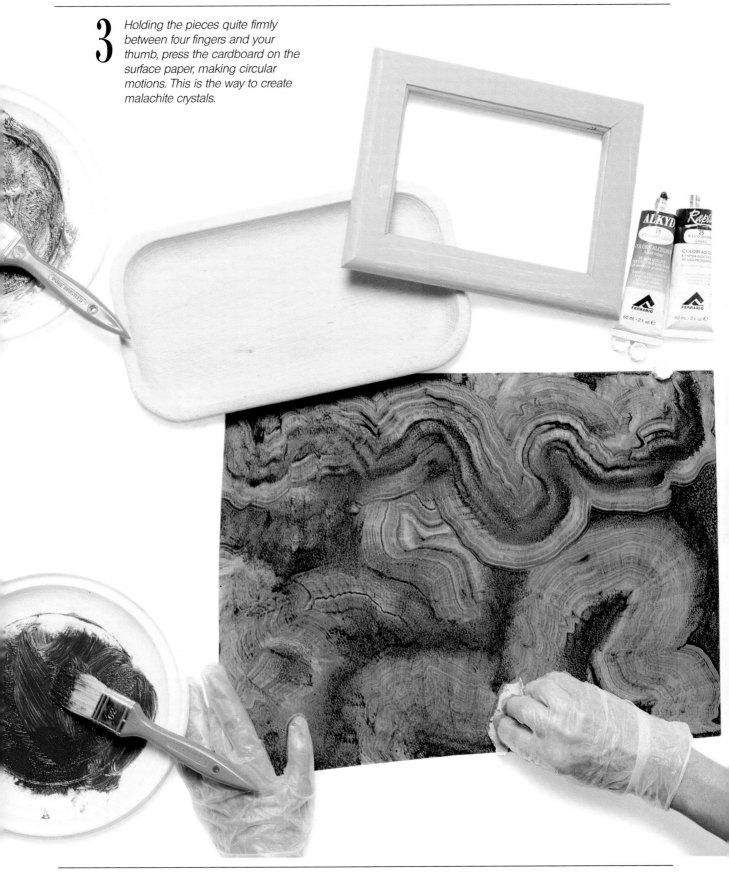

BRICKS AND TERRACOTTA

Bricks and terracotta are amusing objects to copy. Their indefinite color suggests an interesting combination of hues sponged several times one over the other with slightly different shades.

1 Prepare the surface that needs decorating with a neutral color such as biscuit or beige. Using alkyd colors diluted with the appropriate gel, apply the three colors until you get the color of terracotta. To blend in the colors, dot the surface in an irregular fashion with a large, soft paintbrush. The hues we recommend you use are: red earth, Ochre Yellow and Burnt Sienna. Continue laying the three colors one over the other until the colors of the surface are evenly spread.

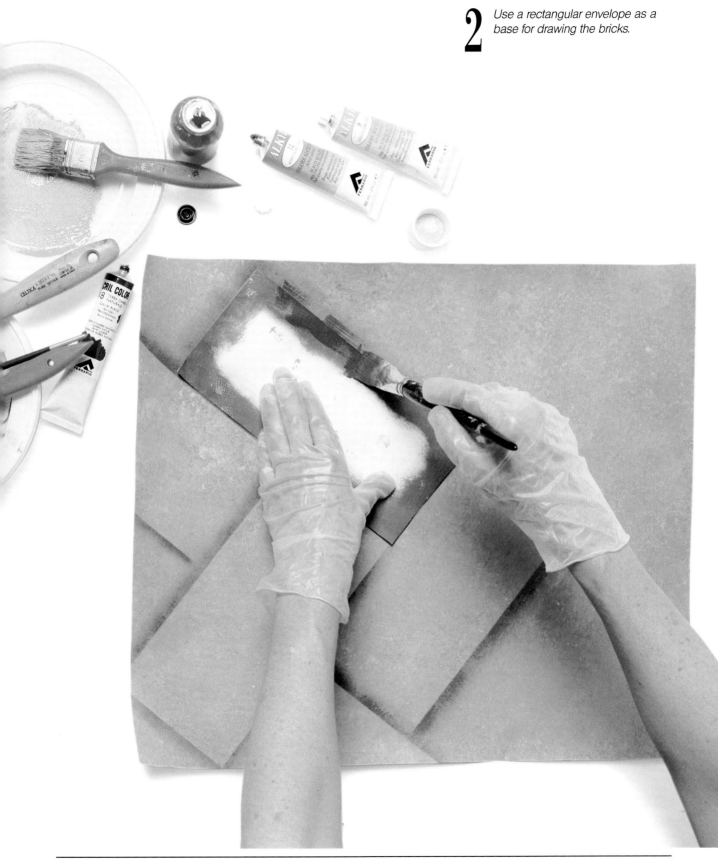

2 *Use a rectangular envelope as a base for drawing the bricks.*

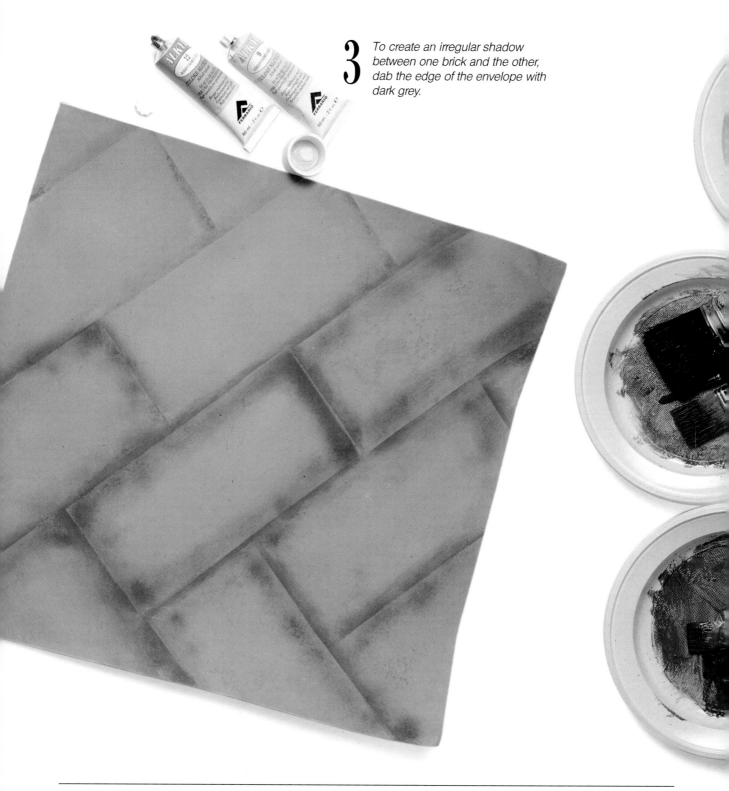

3 To create an irregular shadow between one brick and the other, dab the edge of the envelope with dark grey.

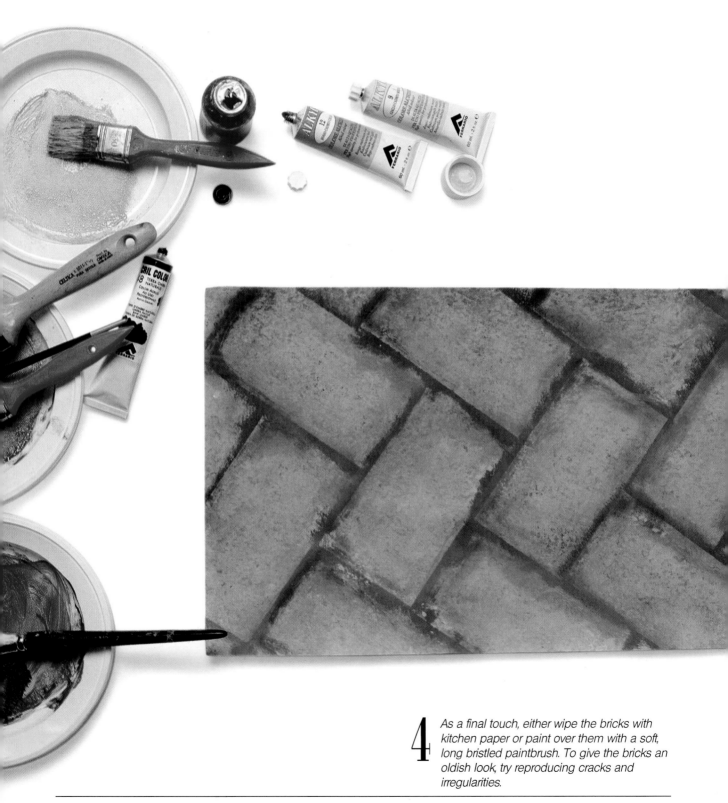

4 As a final touch, either wipe the bricks with
kitchen paper or paint over them with a soft,
long bristled paintbrush. To give the bricks an
oldish look, try reproducing cracks and
irregularities.

ARCHITECTONIC TROMPE L'OEIL

The classical forms of arches, columns, niches, frames or boiseries, more than any other geometric shape, help the artist to create the illusion of space. Even though they are often used as focal points, architectonic structures used in a trompe l'oeil painting require few but very important basic rules.

ARCHES

If the arches lead the eyes of the beholder to the scene beyond the arch itself, the view automatically appears in the foreground, and must therefore be decorated down to the slightest detail. If, instead, the arch itself is the focal point, then it is its very shape and details which must be painted with great precision. In this case, the scene in the background appears as a blurred, or scantily sketched set of elements.

LIGHT

The arch is dark where it curves, light down one side and very light along the side lit by the source of light.

THE VIEW POINT

Frontal: Make the oblique lines inside the arch longer: you will note that they have a point in common, on the horizon line, towards which they all converge: the accidental/focal point.

Accidental: The oblique lines drawn in an accidental perspective do not meet, but cut the scene diagonally only to disappear behind the arch.

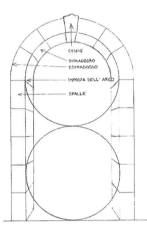

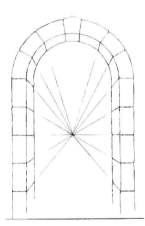

AN ARCH

The three-mullioned Arabian arch, with small cupolas as key points, are the focal point of the drawing on the left. The scene beyond the arch is scantily sketched; the bare branches timidly peeping in from the left are the only point of interest in the whole scene.

NICHES

Niches, like arches, can give the illusion of three dimensionality thanks to clever touches of light and shade in the inside part of the curve.

A deep niche creates soft shadows and therefore calls for greater ability in playing with tones, ranging from the lightest to the darkest ones.

Before starting:

1. Decide at what level you wish to position your niche
2. Decide where the source of light comes from and, according to this, project the shelf within the visual range.

COLUMNS

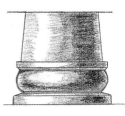

As the frescoes in the houses at Pompeii show, columns appeared in wall decorating during the Roman era. They reappeared in the XIV century thanks to an Italian architect, Andrea Palladio. Today they are considered to be among the most characteristic and elegant elements in early architectonic painting. Columns have a precise role: to support other elements such as an architrave or an arch. If, however, they directly touch the ceiling, their role is that of creating an aseptic atmosphere of spirituality. There exist three main types of columns; Doric, Ionic and Corinthian, which are easily recognizable thanks to the capitals.

Before commencing: Once again, decide where the light comes from. The most illuminated part is obviously the one directly in front of the source of light. The shadows on the column gradually increase, and become very dark

round 2/3 of the curve and then again slightly lighter on the opposite side. To reproduce a colonnade, draw each column as if it were a simple cylinder and then erase the part which is not visible to the eye.

Above: an Ionic capital
Below left: a Doric capital
To the right: a Corinthian capital.

BOISERIES

Boiseries are particularly advisable for decorating the lower part of a wall. In this case, however, to create depth we cannot avail ourselves of the laws of perspective because in boiserie the only "depth" that can be represented is the width of the frame. We are therefore obliged to create the illusion of depth entirely with the chiaroscuro technique.

Before beginning: Study the position of the windows and calculate how much light will be shed on the frame. You will see that two sides of the rectangle will be less illuminated and therefore darker than the other two, which will naturally be more illuminated and therefore lighter.

Marine landscape with boiserie
The illusion of depth created following the instructions outlined above is evident.

PYRAMIDS

Pyramid boiserie is without doubt the most decorative of all, especially if made with pseudo wood.

Light is decreasingly shed on the 4 triangles: from a darker tone, far away from the source of light, to the lighter one, exactly opposite the latter.

EASY
TROMPE L'OEIL

With those of you tackling this technique for the first time in mind, I decided to describe six easy projects, simple to draw and amusing to do. The "step-by-step" explanations which follow have been written using quite simple terminology, so that they may be carried out without too many difficulties.

A LIBRARY

1. These books were drawn as simple, different-sized rectangles, slightly rounded at the top. Of note is the book lying horizontally on top of the others.

2. Attach strips of paper adhesive along the contors of the books, paint in the area with a different color for each volume. Maintain the main colors uniform; you needn't worry about the chiaroscuro effect until later.

3. Once you have painted the books, remove the paper adhesive. Start giving the books their rounded shape. As the source of light is situated on the right, draw a thin white line on the left side of the spine of each book. Always bear in mind the main color of the book: if the spine is black, its shading

must be grey-white; if the background is blue, the shadow must be light bluish white, and so on. Finally, a very dark, almost black line contouring the books will serve to define the part of the spine least illuminated and to create a net division between each book.

4. The library will have in this way acquired volume without the selected main color having been altered. Decorate the books as you will, making some books more particular than others. Some volumes can be standing perfectly straight on the bookshelf, while others could be leaning against another book, either to its left or its right: the areas in between must be darkened to give depth to the shelves.

CLOSET WITH MUSIC SCORE

The door set slightly ajar and the music score only slightly visible over the drawer gives this closet an extraordinary sense of perspective. The first drawing shows how the perspective project was used to create depth of field. Canary yellow, light and dark Burnt Sienna, Yellow Ochre were used to create the extraordinary contrast in this trompe l'oeil painting.

1. Draw the closet, making sure you respect the perspective project. Decide on the focal point, towards which all the perspective lines must converge.

2. Start coloring the closet, making sure you spread the colors evenly. Do not worry about giving the chiaroscuro effect yet. Draw the pentagram and musical notes on the sheet of paper peeping out of the drawer.

3. As you color, create the contrasts. Give the color an artificial wood look, create the shadow beneath the sheet of paper folded over the drawer, and then proceed to darkening both the inside of the drawer and the shelves of the closet, which are only barely visible behind the door.

4. To give the lock a realistic look, lighten the metal grey in the centre and sketch out a very dark shadow starting from the right to the area directly below it.

A BAROQUE PANEL

As you have already seen in the fourth chapter, dusting is a quick way of creating elaborate designs in all their complexity. Sketch the drawing on a large piece of heavy acetate paper and then pierce it along its contours with a pin or needle. Having made many little perforated holes, the outline is consequently "dusted" on the wall.

1. Sponge the surface to decorate with an acrylic color; prepare two hues of the same color: one lighter than the other, and then apply the lighter hue first.

2. Dust the drawing on the surface using a muslin pad filled with black powdered pigment.

3. Prepare four hues of the chosen color:

two lighter and two darker ones. Start spreading the two lighter hues, making sure you carefully follow the trend of the shading.

4. Now pass the two darker tones over the shadowed parts: at this point the image will begin to acquire shape and to "come out" of the background. If the leaves and the vine-tendril do not have sufficient volume, insist slightly with the dark tones.

5. The finished drawing is perfectly balanced. The shape of the leaves and the curls are completely symmetrical. Now work on the left hand side of the drawing and then proceed to repeating the same procedure on the right hand side.

SIENESE VILLA

A gate set slightly ajar leads the eye down a narrow drive lined with evergreen pines, to a characteristic Sienese villa. An inviting image built on the project of a simple frontal perspective. The source of light is situated on the left and casts shadows at a right angle between the two gates.

1. Following the indications on the laws of perspective described in chapter 3, draw the picture with a frontal perspective according to the geometric solid method. The two rows of pines receding towards the focal point stem from the superimposition of the volume of each single tree: the volume is partly hidden by the element preceding it.

2. Start by coloring in the sky, first spreading it evenly with light-blue and then shading in the white, lightning it towards the horizon.

3. To give volume to the sphere on top of the columns, color the surface with at least three different tones of grey. Attach strips of paper adhesive along the gate and columns. Using the same tones, create the boiserie effect and give three dimensionality to the gate.

4. To obtain the pebble effect on the drive, sponge Ochre Yellow, grey and white one over the other. Use a ruler and set square to create the shadows between the two gates at 90°.

5. Finally, to give the illusion of sun rays filtering through the branches, use white in between the pines in the left row.

MARBLED NICHE

A niche marbled in dark blue discreetly highlights a colorful flower vase. The brilliant pink and bright yellow used for the flowers stand out against the dark marble. Note how at the two ends the light points give rise to a protruding effect; the dark shadows inside the niche, instead, trick the eye, giving the impression of space behind the vase of flowers.

1. Draw the niche by marking the central axis of the drawing. Decide on the depth of the shelf, calculating the protrusion of the sill. Draw the bouquet of flowers and the vase, positioning the drawing on the central axis.

2. Marble the niche and color the flowers, harmonising the shapes and colors. With a fine tipped paintbrush, reproduce the veins on the petals and leaves. Respect the contrasts: the small sill casts a shadow directly below it, while the glass vase is lighter down both its sides.

AN ORNAMENTAL BOUQUET

This fresh bouquet, created in true pictorial style, gives an almost naïf effect. The light/dark nuances of green divide the leaves from each other, which makes it easy to arrange them artistically among the flowers. Observe the position of the outer flowers, turned leftwards and rightwards: a trick which creates a sensation of volume for the sphere.

1. On a piece of plywood, draw and then cut out a bouquet of flowers as if ideally contained in a round shape. Outline the vase under this explosion of petals and leaves.

2. Color the bouquet, playing with light and dark hues upon the petals according to their position.

The knick-knack bouquet, created to adorn a piece of furniture, may also be used as a shade for a lamp.

SCENIC
TROMPE L'OEIL

A WINDOW OVERLOOKING THE WOODLANDS

Window frames, like boiseries and chair shields, can be very convincing. The illusion created by this window owes a lot to the correct shading of the frame, which goes from light to very dark tones, passing through medium and dark ones, each one seen on a different level.

WINDOW WITH CREEPERS

This small window, its shutters closed, is partly hidden by a creeper. Observe the light and dark nuances created by the leaves overlapping one another and by the soft shadows cast by the small pyramids situated around the window.

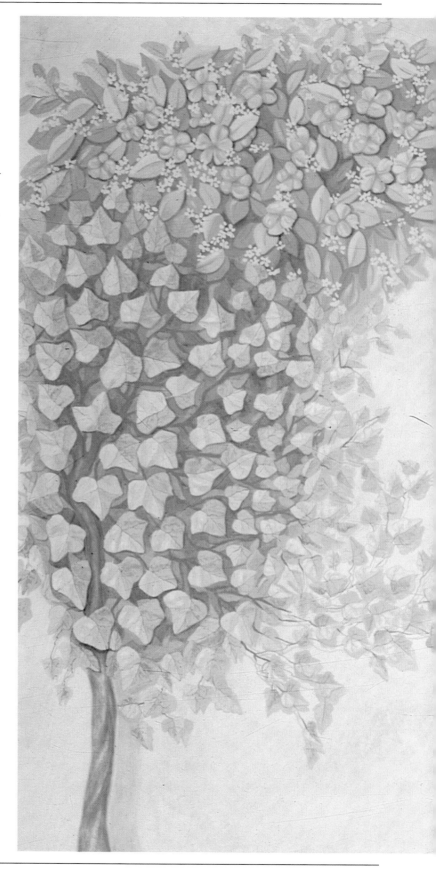

WARDROBE DECORATED BY THE DUSTING TECHNQUE

Painting furniture became the rage in the Venetian region in the 19th century. Since then, decorated wardrobes and chests of drawers have represented the most important pieces of furniture in many fashionable living rooms. The dusting technique is therefore also suitable for decorating furniture.

DRY FLOWERS ADORNING A CHEST OF DRAWERS

A composition depicting dry flowers in a terracotta vase and bunches of flowers symmetrically arranged to hang from a festoon stand out against the dark green background and enliven a simple chest of drawers. The scene seems to be painted on a door which almost entirely hides the five drawers.

A STILL LIFE WARDROBE

Take a plate rack and a library as a subject and the "picture" effect obtained on the wardrobe doors was achieved through the use of the traditional pictorial method known as "still life", through the use of oil colors and a diluting agent. Given that the objects are simply seen one in front of the other, no specific perspective project is necessary to give the impression of space. The dark area behind the objects looks like an evenly spread shadow, typical of still life painting.

A RABBIT'S CAGE

The shape of this chest of drawers lends itself perfectly to painting rabbits in their cage. The animals are painted behind two wire-nettings more or less situated on the same level. The light comes from the left and falls on the right, illuminating the silvery white patches of the rabbits and creating a semi-dark effect at the back of the cage.

A FLORAL SREEN

A wide mahogany sideboard separates the night area from the living room, and this floral screen gives it a touch of fantasy and color.

The plants vary slightly in their tones and hues. The vases accentuate the illusion of near and far because they appear on different levels thanks to both careful nuancing and to the fact that the doors of the screen are adjusted at different angles.

ARTIST'S TROMPE L'OEIL

Gabriella Gallerani is a versatile and refined artist: from fashion to advertising graphics, from scientific illustrations to creative "restoration" of pieces of old furniture, her works are a blend of observation, reflection, and memory.

Gabriella Gallerani prefers depicting the world of nature and animals, which she reproduces with an extremely fine precision and realism, which usually only a camera lens can give. Furnishing a small house in the country becomes almost a game, and old pieces of furniture in her hands become fully fledged creations of art, almost always "adorned" with small animals.

Depicted on the left is a clove of garlic hanging from what appears to be a small closet but which is really no more than the door of the closet itself. The interior reveals two glass vials and a frightened cat looking out from behind the bars.
A few ivy leaves creeping up from the bottle add movement to this austere painting.
Size: 37x46x5

A strange theme was chosen to decorate the door of this closet: half a dozen opium chalices. The artist created with great realism the selected subject without exaggerating with the colors or the contrasts. Inside the closet, arranged on three shelves, are a heap of dusty bottles. The translucent effect obtained and which reveal the light/dark parts of the blown glass was achieved by mixing vynavil with greyish white tempera.
Size: 32x51x10.

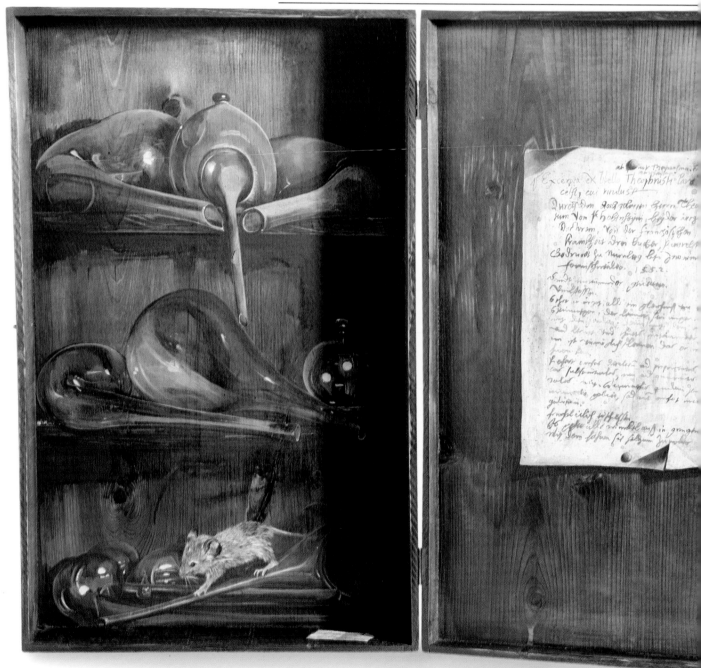

The hollow door of this closet loses its flat two-dimensionality and acquires a deep cavity hosting a glass vase with an orhid placed behind some wire-netting. The artist first drew the object in the "cavity" and only later painted in the wire.
Size: 44,5 x 14.

A profusion of ivy leaves "grows" across this rudimental, unusual cat carrier. The artist drew leaves overlapping one another, giving greater importance to the fresh green leaves which strongly contrast with the slightly yellowed and dry ones.

This unusual half open jewel casket reveals its contents: a rose, some dry leaves, a piece of crumpled paper, a string of pearls. Observe carefully: the box is really closed; the rest is merely an illusion created by the artist.
Size: 22,5 x 17,3 x 6.

An insignificant box with a flap back double opening is adorned with insects and flower prints. Take particular note of the very dark color, obtained with Umber and black, used to decorate the insects, whose shapes are clearly visible against the dark wood. Two points of light skilfully painted on the back of the insects give their bodies volume. Size: 30 x 12 x 11,5.

This solitary pigeon, ready to take flight, looks out of the wire-netting. Clever shades of neutral pinkish and greenish greys were used to color the composition.
Size: 36 x 26,5 x 10.

This old, picturesque trunk was adorned with a ramage of yellow orchids which contrast sharply with the dark wood. The ramage does not seem to notice the handle or the lock, but appears to creep up from behind these obstacles.

The incongruous collection of objects on these shelves are a proof of the artist's skill: the translucent quality of the silver objects is rendered extremely well. The soft chiaroscuro plush effect is highlighted in the mouse while the old volume on the top shelf gives the perfect idea of something dated and second hand. Behind the mouse is an old wedding photograph worn with time. The same technique which consists in mixing vinavyl with tempera colors was used to give a silvery quality to some objects as well as to paint the glass of the photo frame.
Size: 45x36x0,8

Curious and sinister at the same time, two owls wink behind a wire-netting.
Size: 35x45x17,5

The elegant vials are nuanced differently according to their position. The long bottle in the foreground appears clean and transparent, while the bottles arranged in the background are tarnished and darkened by an internal shadow. A large toad is sitting in the foreground, distinctly lit by the source of light coming from the right.

TROMPE L'OEIL IMAGES

This section shows various drawings and details that can be reproduced by making photocopies. They can be used following the different techniques outlined in this manual to help the artist to create trompe l'oeil according to his/her personal needs.

152

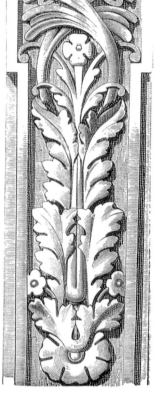

INDEX